Hot and Bright

A Book About the Sun

by Dana Meachen Rau   illustrated by Denise Shea

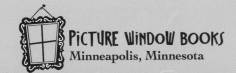

PICTURE WINDOW BOOKS
Minneapolis, Minnesota

Thanks to our advisers for their expertise, research, and advice:

Dr. Stanley P. Jones, Assistant Director
NASA-sponsored Classroom of the Future Program

Susan Kesselring, M.A., Literacy Educator
Rosemount–Apple Valley–Eagan (Minnesota) School District

Editorial Director: Carol Jones
Managing Editor: Catherine Neitge
Creative Director: Keith Griffin
Editor: Christianne Jones
Story Consultant: Terry Flaherty
Designer: Joe Anderson
Page Production: Picture Window Books
The illustrations in this book were created digitally.

Picture Window Books
5115 Excelsior Boulevard
Suite 232
Minneapolis, MN 55416
877-845-8392
www.picturewindowbooks.com

Printed in the United States of America.

Library of Congress Cataloging-in-Publication Data
Rau, Dana Meachen, 1971-
Hot and bright : a book about the sun / by Dana Meachen Rau ; illustrated by Denise Shea.
p. cm. — (Amazing science)
Includes bibliographical references and index.
ISBN 1-4048-1135-4 (hardcover)
ISBN 1-4048-1730-1 (paperback)
1. Sun—Juvenile literature. 2. Heat—Juvenile literature. 3. Light—Juvenile literature.
I. Shea, Denise, ill. II. Title. III. Series.

QB521.5.R35 2006
523.7—dc22
2005003726

Table of Contents

SUNSCREEN

SPF 45

The Closest Star

Look up at the sky on a clear night. There are many stars. Have you ever tried to count them? There are too many stars to count!

Now, count the stars you can see during the day. There is just one—the closest one. This star is our sun.

FUN FACT

You cannot see the sun on a
cloudy day, but it is always there.

Our Solar System

The sun is a middle-sized star. It looks big to you because it is so close to Earth.

It is the center of our solar system. Our solar system is made up of the sun and nine planets.

FUN FACT

The sun is the largest object in our solar system. All nine planets move around the sun.

Sun and Movement

Where is the sun when you wake up? Where is the sun at noon? Where is the sun at dinnertime? The sun seems to move across the sky. However, the sun is not really moving around Earth. Earth is turning as it is moves around the sun.

FUN FACT

Earth makes one trip around the sun every 365 days. That's why we have 365 days in a year.

A Giant Top

Earth spins like a giant toy top. The sun's light can only shine on half of Earth at a time. When you are on the lit side of Earth, it is day. When you are on the dark side, it is night. Earth's spinning makes the sun seem to appear and disappear.

FUN FACT

Sometimes, our moon blocks our view of the sun and you see a solar eclipse. During a solar eclipse, you can see the sun's light peeking out around the edge of the moon.

Light and Heat

You might sit in front of a fireplace on a cold winter night. The fire gives off light. It also gives off heat. The sun is like a fireplace. The sun gives off light and heat, too. It is much hotter than a fireplace.

FUN FACT

The sun's heat is so hot that we can feel it from 93 million miles (150 million kilometers) away. That is how far Earth is from the sun.

Sunspots and Solar Flares

The sun often has black dots that move across its surface. The dots are called sunspots. The sun may also have shooting flames. The shooting flames are called solar flares. They are explosions on the surface of the sun. They occur near sunspots.

FUN FACT

In just a matter of minutes, solar flares heat up to millions of degrees. They release as much energy as a billion megatons of dynamite.

The Sun and You

We could not live without the sun. Its heat keeps us warm. We also need its light to see. Earth would be very dark and cold without the sun.

FUN FACT

The sun helps plants make their own food. Sunlight hits a plant's leaves. Tiny green parts in the leaves change the sunlight into plant food.

Earth's Tilt

What makes Earth feel cold in winter?
What makes Earth feel hot in summer?
The sun does! It makes the seasons.

Earth is tilted. The part that is tilted toward
the sun gets more of the sun's heat. The
people in this area have summer. The
part that is tilted away from the sun has
winter. As Earth moves around the sun,
the seasons change.

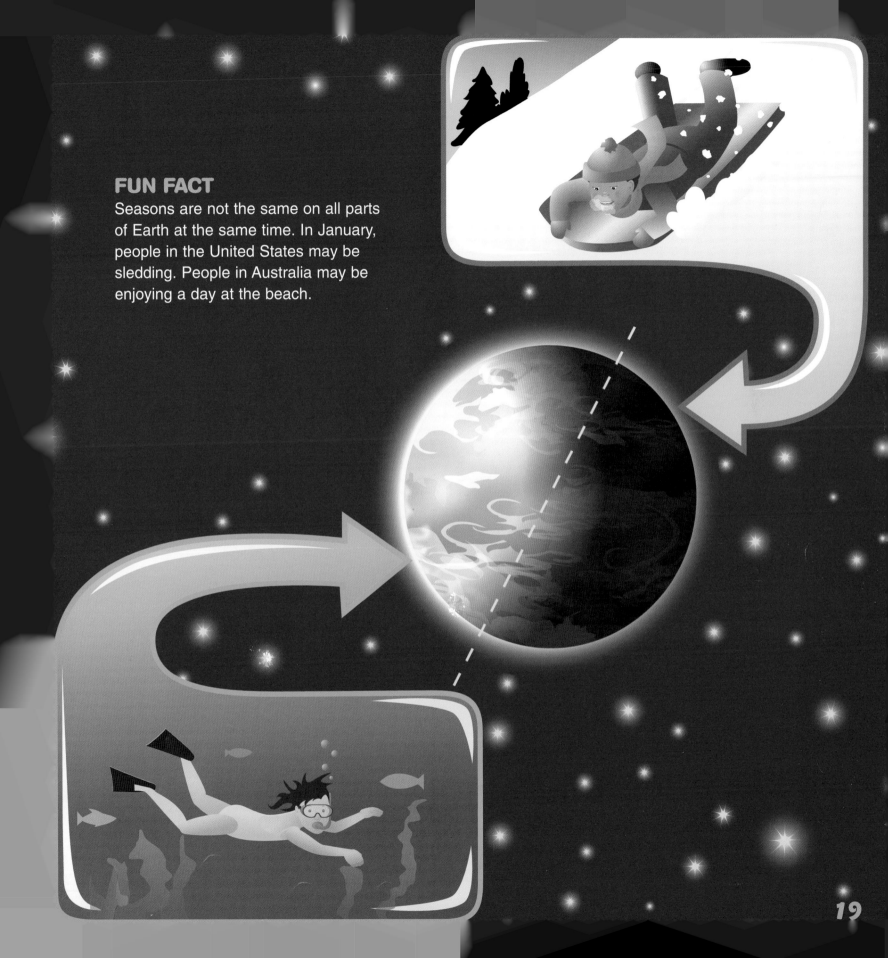

FUN FACT

Seasons are not the same on all parts
of Earth at the same time. In January,
people in the United States may be
sledding. People in Australia may be
enjoying a day at the beach.

Harmful Rays

We need the sun, but the sun's rays can hurt us.
Have you ever stayed out in the sunlight too long?
Did your skin turn red?

The sun's rays are so strong that they can burn your skin.
You need to put on sunscreen to protect your skin. Then
you can go out to play. Protect yourself, and the sun will
brighten your day.

FUN FACT

Never look directly at the sun. The sun's light is too bright. It could burn your eyes.

Changing Shadows

What you need:
* sidewalk chalk
* a friend
* a sunny day

What you do:

1. Choose a day when it is going to be sunny all day long. In the morning, find a flat, clear area, such as a driveway or sidewalk.

2. Draw a line on the ground. Have your friend stand on the line. Be sure the sun is behind him or her.

3. Trace your friend's shadow with the sidewalk chalk.

4. Go out again in the middle of the day. Have your friend stand on the line and trace the shadow again with a different color chalk.

5. Go out at the end of the day, and trace the shadow again with a third color of chalk.

6. How did the shadow change throughout the day? Did it get longer or shorter? Did it move or stay in the same place?

Sunny Facts

An Old Star
People who study the sun think it's between 4.5 and 5 billion years old.

Just Right for Life
There is life on Earth because it is just the right distance from the sun. If Earth were closer to the sun, Earth would be too hot for life. If it were farther away, it would be too cold.

Pretty Pictures
It is not safe to look directly at the sun. One way people study the sun is by looking at pictures. The pictures are taken by spaceships that study the sun.

Shadow Games
Shadows change their shape throughout the day. When the sun is high in the sky, your shadow will look short. When the sun is low, your shadow will look long.

One of Many
The sun is just one star among the billions of stars in space. Groups of stars in space are called galaxies. There are billions of galaxies, too!

Glossary

galaxy—a large group of stars, planets, and other matter, such as dust and gas
solar flares—shooting flames coming out of the sun
solar system—a star and the planets that circle around it
star—a ball of burning gas
sunscreen—a cream that you put on your skin to protect it from the sun's harmful rays
sunspots—dark, cool spots on the sun
top—a toy that's shaped like a cone and spins

To Learn More

At the Library

Bailey, Jacqui. *Sun Up, Sun Down: The Story of Day and Night*. Minneapolis: Picture Window Books, 2004.

Branley, Franklyn M. *The Sun: Our Nearest Star*. New York: HarperCollins, 2002.

Tocci, Salvatore. *Experiments with the Sun and the Moon*. New York: Children's Press, 2003.

On the Web

FactHound offers a safe, fun way to find Web sites related to this book. All of the sites on FactHound have been researched by our staff.

1. Visit *www.facthound.com*
2. Type in this special code: 1404811354
3. Click on the FETCH IT button.

Your trusty FactHound will fetch the best Web sites for you!

www.FactHound.com

Look for all of the books in the Amazing Science: Exploring the Sky series:

Fluffy, Flat, and Wet: A Book About Clouds
Hot and Bright: A Book About the Sun
Night Light: A Book About the Moon
Space Leftovers: A Book About Comets, Asteroids, and Meteoroids
Spinning in Space: A Book About the Planets
Spots of Light: A Book About Stars